Spiders

CLAIRE LLEWELLYN • BARRIE WATTS

W
FRANKLIN WATTS
A Division of Scholastic Inc.
NEW YORK TORONTO LONDON AUCKLAND SYDNEY
MEXICO CITY NEW DELHI HONG KONG
DANBURY, CONNECTICUT

First published in 2000 by Franklin Watts
96 Leonard Street, London EC2A 4XD

First American edition 2002 by Franklin Watts
A Division of Scholastic Inc.
90 Sherman Turnpike
Danbury, CT 06816

Series Editor: Anderley Moore
Editor: Rosalind Beckman
Series Designer: Jason Anscomb
Illustrator: David Burroughs

Catalog details are available from the Library of Congress
Cataloging-in-Publication Data

ISBN 0-531-14652-9 (lib. bdg.) 0-531-14827-0 (pbk.)

Printed in Hong Kong/China

Contents

Spiders' Bodies

Spiders live all over the world. There are thousands of different kinds of spiders, but they all have the same shaped body.

The crab spider is as small as your little fingernail.

Spiders are members of an animal family called arachnids. They can be big or small, but they all have eight legs.

The Goliath tarantula is as big as a frisbee.

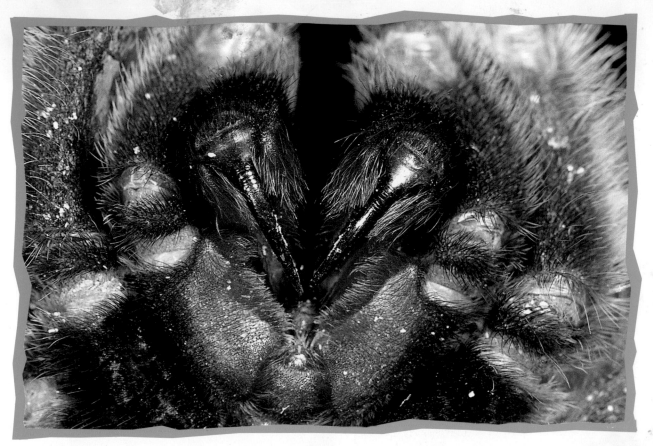

A spider's fangs are poisonous and sharp.

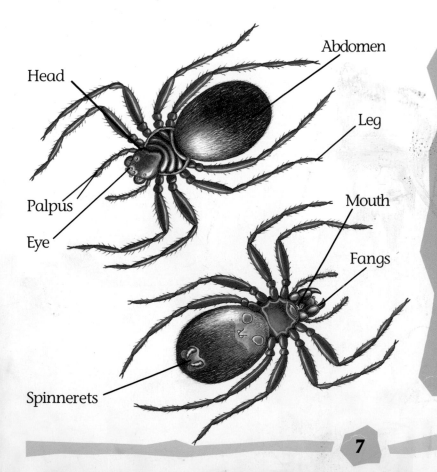

Head

Palpus

Eye

Abdomen

Leg

Mouth

Fangs

Spinnerets

A spider's body is split into two parts: the head and the abdomen. On the head are its legs, fangs, and two palpi. Palpi help the spider taste and feel. On the abdomen are spinnerets, which make silk for spinning webs.

Spider Skin

Spiders have a tough coat that protects their bodies and gives them their shape. This thick coat is called the exoskeleton.

The exoskeleton covers every part of a spider's body, even its eyes.

The Chilean rose tarantula has a hairy body. All spiders have some hairs on their body.

Shedding skin

❶ The exoskeleton that a spider is born with does not grow with the spider. In time, it begins to feel tight and splits open.

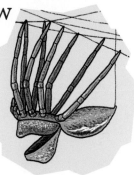

As soon as the spider's skin has hardened, the spider crawls away and leaves its old coat behind. The picture below is of an empty old spider skin.

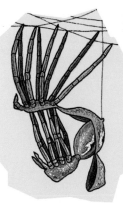

❷ The spider pulls itself out of the old skin. Underneath is a new, larger skin.

❸ The spider's new skin is soft like jelly. It takes a few hours to harden in the air.

Spider Silk

Spiders dangle from a thread that is finer than hair, but much stronger and very stretchy. The thread is called silk. Spiders use silk to make their webs, trap their prey, and protect their eggs.

Silk oozes out of the spinnerets. Spiders pull it out with their legs to make long, hard threads.

Spiders use their webs to catch insects. As soon as an insect flies into a web, the spider feels the silk shake.

Making a Web

The orb spider spins a round web.

A spider's web is a deadly trap for catching flies and other insects. The fine, lacy threads can be ruined by dust, rain, or wind. Most spiders spin a new web every night. Webs take about an hour to make.

❶ The spider makes a strong thread between two twigs.

❷ Then it makes a second, looser thread and pulls it down.

*Not all webs are round. This one is shaped like a triangle.
It is found in the grass. It is made by the money spider.*

❸ The spider adds more spokes and fixes them firmly.

❹ A sticky, spiral thread holds all the spokes in place.

Catching a Meal

When an insect flies into a spider's web, it gets stuck in the sticky threads. The spider runs over, bites the insect with its poisonous fangs, then wraps it up tightly in silk. A spider often saves its meals for later.

A spider waits in its web for an insect to land. It stays very still.

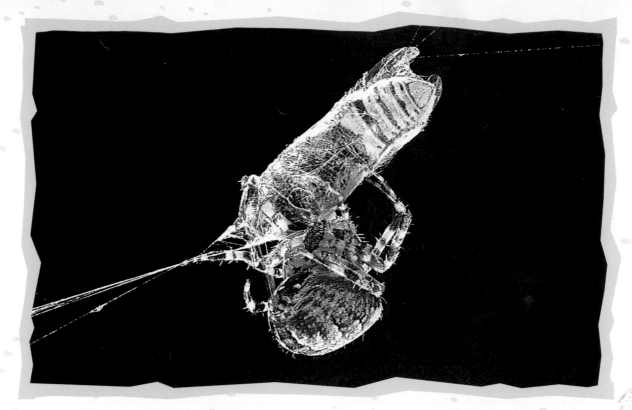

A garden spider wraps up a wasp. A spider can store several insect meals in its web.

Spiders have such small mouths that they can only eat food that is runny. The poison they stick into their prey changes its body into a kind of soup. The spider sucks up the soup.

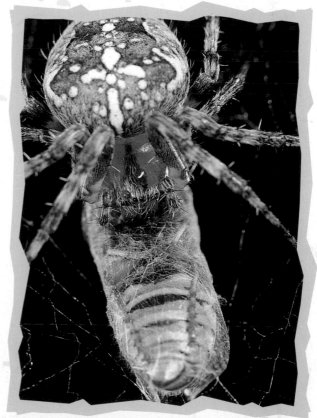

Hunters

Many spiders do not spin webs. They hunt for their food instead. Hunting spiders are strong and fast. They have good eyesight to spot their prey.

The Mexican redknee spider is a deadly hunter.

The zebra spider has two large eyes that help it find tiny creatures. The spider pounces and pins them down, then bites them with its fangs.

Silk shooter

The bolas spider hunts for its food by throwing out a line of sticky silk. It swings the silk around like a cowboy's lasso to catch insects as they fly by.

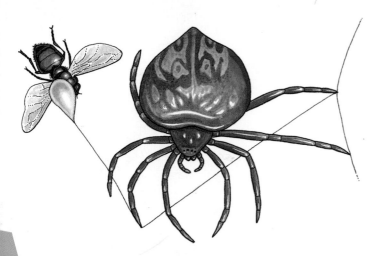

Poison spitter

The spitting spider stalks its prey like a cat. When the spider gets close, it fires a sticky poison from its fangs, pinning its meal to the ground.

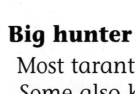

Big hunter

Most tarantulas eat insects. Some also kill larger animals, such as frogs, lizards, snakes, and chicks!

Hiding

Some spiders are sneaky hunters. They ambush their prey. They hide somewhere safe and wait for an insect. As soon as a tasty meal comes near, they jump out and grab it

Some spiders hide under the ground to ambush their prey. The trapdoor spider makes a burrow with a trapdoor on the top. At night, it opens the door a crack to look for passing insects.

The crab spider hides inside flowers, where it catches visiting insects. The insects do not see the spider because it can change its color to match the flower. The spider also stays very still.

The purse-web spider makes a silk tube on the ground, and covers it with soil. The spider hides inside the tube. It stabs passing insects through the soft wall and drags them inside the tube.

Finding a Mate

A male spider must find a female mate to make baby spiderlings. To attract a female, the male spider gives her an insect, visits her web, or waves his legs around. If she accepts him, the two spiders mate.

A male spider is smaller than a female spider.

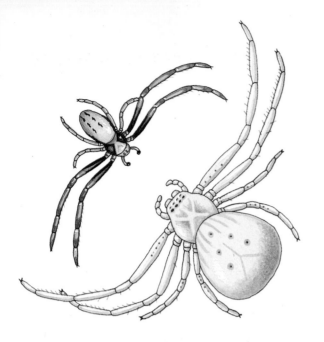

During mating, a male spider has to be careful. The female is bigger than he is, and she might eat him by mistake!

Female spiders lay eggs in a soft bag of silk called a sac. This garden spider dies soon afterward.

Spiderlings

Most female spiders leave their egg sacs on fences or trees. Next spring, the eggs hatch into tiny spiderlings. The spiderlings need to spread out to find food. They each make a line of silk and float away on the breeze.

The nursery web spider does not leave her egg sac behind. She carries it around with her until the eggs hatch.

These spiderlings have just hatched out of their sac. Soon each one will go its own way. ▶

Escaping Danger

Spiders make a juicy meal for animals such as birds, lizards, toads, and wasps. Most spiders escape from danger by dropping down on a line of silk. Others attack their enemies.

Hunting wasps are a wolf spider's greatest enemy. Wasps dig up the burrows where the spider hides. When it sees an enemy, the spider rises up on its legs and shows its fangs.

A bird-eating spider attacks its enemies by brushing its hair onto them. The spider's hairs have sharp little hooks. The hooks stick into the enemy's skin and make it feel itchy and sore.

Spidery Snippets

Spiders can be dangerous. In some places, they kill more people than snakes do.

A black widow spider is about fifteen times more poisonous than a rattlesnake.

A spider can go without food for many months.

The remains of ancient spiders have been found inside drops of sticky sap.

About 300 years ago, a Frenchman used spider silk to make stockings and gloves.

Spiders are ancient creatures. The first ones lived on Earth about 400 million years ago.

A jumping spider can leap forty times the length of its body. That is like a person jumping the length of three tennis courts.

The web of the golden orb spider measures more than 6 feet across. Some people use it as a fishing net.

Spiders are a farmer's friend. They eat many harmful insects.

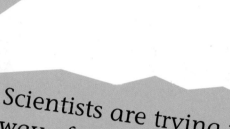

Scientists are trying to find a way of making a poison just like a spider's. This could be used on farm crops to kill harmful insects, without harming birds or the soil.

A jumping spider's eyes are bigger than its brain.

There are one thousand spider eggs in an egg sac the size of a pea.

Glossary

abdomen	the back part of a spider's body
ambush	to hide and wait for an attack
arachnid	an animal that has eight legs, two body parts, and an exoskeleton
exoskeleton	the hard outer coat that protects the body of spiders and many other animals
fangs	the sharp claws that spiders use to bite and poison their prey
insect	an animal that has six legs and three parts to its body
palpus	a feeler on a spider's head that helps it taste and feel (plural: palpi)
prey	an animal that is hunted by another animal for food
sac	the bag of silk that holds a spider's eggs
spinneret	the part of a spider's body that lets out silk for making webs

Index